09

# Desert Animals

Written by DEBORAH HODGE
Illustrated by PAT STEPHENS

Kids Can Press

**For Mike, a desert adventurer, who mountain biked in Moab
and rock climbed in Joshua Tree – D.H.**

**For Caitlin – P.S.**

I would like to gratefully acknowledge the expert review of the manuscript and art by Dr. Judith L. Eger, Senior Curator of Mammals, Department of Natural History, Royal Ontario Museum, Toronto, Ontario.

Thank you also to my hardworking editors Lisa Tedesco and Sheila Barry
for their continuing advice and support.

---

Text © 2008 Deborah Hodge
Illustrations © 2008 Pat Stephens

Kids Can Press acknowledges the financial support of the Government of Ontario, through the Ontario Media Development Corporation's Ontario Book Initiative; the Ontario Arts Council; the Canada Council for the Arts; and the Government of Canada, through the BPIDP, for our publishing activity.

Published in Canada by
Kids Can Press Ltd.
29 Birch Avenue
Toronto, ON  M4V 1E2

Published in the U.S. by
Kids Can Press Ltd.
2250 Military Road
Tonawanda, NY  14150

www.kidscanpress.com

Kids Can Press is a *Corus*™ Entertainment company

Edited by Lisa Tedesco and Sheila Barry
Designed by Kathleen Gray
Printed and bound in Singapore

The paper used to print this book was produced with elemental chlorine-free pulp, harvested from managed sustainable forests.

The hardcover edition of this book is smyth sewn casebound. The paperback edition of this book is limp sewn with a drawn-on cover.

CM 08  0 9 8 7 6 5 4 3 2 1
CM PA 08  0 9 8 7 6 5 4 3 2 1

**Library and Archives Canada Cataloguing in Publication**
Hodge, Deborah
    Desert animals / written by Deborah Hodge ;
illustrated by Pat Stephens.

(Who lives here?)
ISBN 978-1-55453-047-2 (bound)
ISBN 978-1-55453-048-9 (pbk.)

1. Desert animals—Juvenile literature. I. Stephens, Pat, 1950–
II. Title. III. Series: Hodge, Deborah. Who lives here?

QL116.H63 2008          j591.754          C2007-905565-6

# Contents

# What Is a Desert?

A desert is a very dry place. Almost no rain falls here. Most deserts are found in hot parts of the world, under a blazing sun. Deserts can be sandy or rocky. Only a few are cold.

Deserts are home to many interesting animals. Their bodies are built for living in hot places, where there is very little water to drink.

When rain finally falls, beautiful plants and flowers spring up. Small animals nibble on their seeds.

Desert plants, like this cactus, don't need much water. Insects and birds sip sweet juice, called nectar, from its flowers. Mmm!

Many deserts are so hot that small animals must find shade under rocks or shrubs or below the ground.

# Fennec Fox

The fennec fox lives near desert sand hills, called dunes. These furry foxes are the size of small dogs.

Tiny fox pups are born in an underground den. The mother cares for her babies while the father hunts for food.

The fox digs a hole in the sand called a burrow. It hides here during the heat of the day. Whew!

A fox hunts in the cool desert night. It pounces on its prey — the jerboas and other small animals it eats.

Sharp hearing helps a fox find its prey. The big ears also give off heat to keep the fox cool.

# Elf Owl

The elf owl is one of the smallest owls in the world.
Elf owls live in deserts where cactus and shrubs grow.

A mother elf owl makes a cozy nest in an old woodpecker hole
inside a giant cactus. She lays her eggs in this shady spot.

Tiny baby owls hatch from the eggs. The father brings food back to the nest for them.

Whoosh! An elf owl grabs insects in midair with its sharp claws, called talons.

A frightened elf owl covers its light chest with a dark wing. This helps it blend in with its surroundings and hide from enemies.

9

# Sidewinder

The sidewinder is a rattlesnake that slithers sideways across the desert. Sidewinders live in open, sandy places.

The sidewinder's thick, flattened body and rough scales grip the loose sand and help the snake move quickly and easily.

Large scales fold down and protect a sidewinder's eyes when it burrows into the sand.

A sidewinder shakes its rattle to warn enemies away. The rattle makes a buzzing sound. Bzz …

The sidewinder uses its long hollow teeth, called fangs, to hunt small animals. The fangs give a poisonous bite!

11

# Addax

The addax wanders across hot, sandy deserts searching for tasty grasses and shrubs to eat.

Addaxes travel in small groups. They get all their water from the plants they eat and almost never drink. Munch, munch!

Short, white fur reflects the sun's rays and keeps the addax from getting too hot.

Big, flat hooves work like snowshoes to keep the addax from sinking into the sand.

The addax roams the desert in the cool morning and evening. It rests at midday when the sun is hottest. Zzz ...

# Sand Cat

The sand cat prowls over sandy or rocky deserts. These shy, wild cats look like small pet cats.

Sand cats live alone, except for mothers with babies. The tiny kittens are born in a burrow or among rocks. Purr...

14

Long, thick fur on the bottom of a sand cat's paws keep its feet from burning on the hot sand.

The color of the cat's fur blends in with the sand. This helps it sneak up on its prey. Shh …

This hungry cat hunts jerboas, birds and even snakes! Sand cats get all the water they need from their food.

# Scorpion

The desert hairy scorpion lives in cactus deserts. It hides during the hot day and hunts in the cool night.

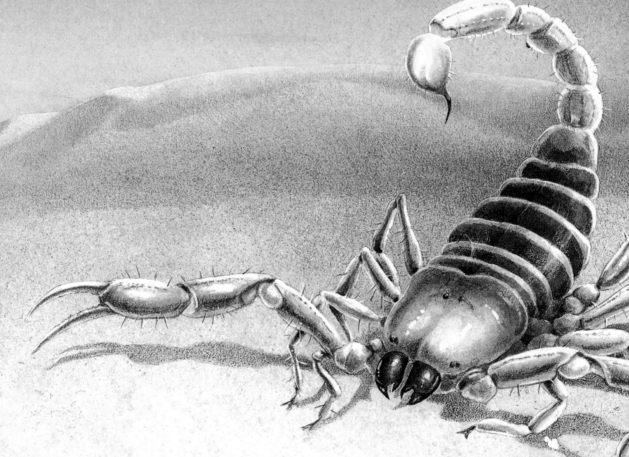

A scorpion has tiny body hairs that sense movement and help it find prey. It grabs insects and spiders with its powerful claws, called pincers.

A scorpion poisons lizards and snakes by plunging its needle-sharp stinger into them. Ouch!

Tiny baby scorpions ride on their mother's back. They are safer here from birds, bats and other enemies.

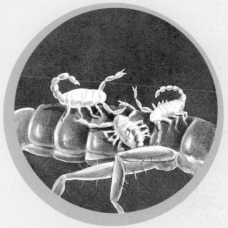

As a scorpion grows, it sheds the tough body covering that is now too tight. A bigger covering has grown underneath.

# Bactrian Camel

The Bactrian camel roams across mountain deserts that have scorching summers and freezing cold winters.

During the winter, a camel's fur works like a warm, woolly blanket to keep out the cold. Much of the fur is shed in summer.

Fat inside a camel's humps keeps it alive when tasty shrubs are hard to find.

A camel can go days without drinking. When it finds water, it drinks enough to fill a bathtub. Slurp!

A camel can close its nostrils to keep blowing sand out of its nose. Long eyelashes protect its eyes.

# Gila Monster

The Gila monster lives on rocky hillsides in cactus deserts. These large lizards have a poisonous bite.

Gila monsters use their tongues to taste the ground and air. This helps them find their prey — the small animals and birds they eat.

This hungry Gila monster has found a nest full of bird's eggs. It will gobble them up. Crunch!

Brightly colored scales on the lizard's body warn enemies to stay away or they might get bitten!

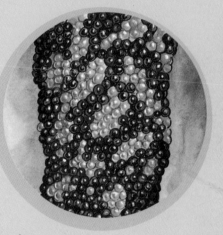

Strong legs and sharp claws help the lizard dig a burrow. Gila monsters spend much of their time underground.

# Roadrunner

The roadrunner is a big bird that runs instead of flies. Roadrunners live near desert bushes and shrubs.

A mother roadrunner builds her nest in a thorny bush or cactus. The parents take turns sitting on the eggs until they hatch.

A roadrunner uses its powerful beak to hunt insects, snakes and lizards. It feeds this prey to its babies.

Long legs help a roadrunner run fast enough to chase its prey and escape its enemies. Zoom!

After a cool night, a roadrunner warms up by turning its back to the sun and sunbathing. Ahh …

# Animal Words

Every desert animal has special body parts that help it get food and stay safe and cool. Can you find pictures of these body parts in the book?

**ear**
page 7

**fangs**
page 11

**fur**
page 13

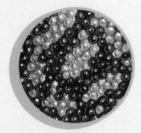
**scales**
page 21

**stinger**
page 17

**talons**
page 9

## For Parents and Teachers

Deserts are the driest places on Earth, receiving less than 250 mm (10 in.) of rain per year. Most are located in or near the Tropics. These deserts have high daytime temperatures, cold nights and very strong winds. The animals that live there are well adapted to such extreme conditions. The fennec fox and sand cat live in the hot Sahara (North Africa) and Arabian Deserts. The addax is also found in the Sahara. The Bactrian camel lives in the cool Gobi Desert in Central Asia. The rest of the animals in this book are from deserts of the American Southwest and northern Mexico.

Deserts are fragile ecosystems that are easily damaged by human activities, such as driving on desert land or building homes and roads. Water becomes even more scarce and plants are harmed, resulting in less food for the animals. Some species, such as the addax, have become endangered. Today, laws are being passed to protect deserts and their species.